AFTERNOON TEA RECIPES

Sian Llewellyn

DOMINO BOOKS (WALES) LTD

METRIC/IMPERIAL/AMERICAN UNITS

We are all used to doubling or halving a recipe. Thus, a Victoria sandwich may be made using 4 oz each of flour, sugar and butter with 2 eggs or 6 oz each of flour, sugar and butter with 3 eggs. The proportions of the ingredients are unchanged. This must be so for all units. Use either the metric units or the imperial units given in the recipes, do not mix the two.

It is not practical to give the exact equivalents of metric and imperial units because 1 oz equals 28.35 g and 1 pint equals 568 ml. The tables on page 47 indicate suitable quantities but liquids should be carefully added to obtain the correct consistency. See also the charts on page iv.

PINTS TO MILLILITRES AND LITRES
The following are approximations only

$\frac{1}{4}$ pint = 150 ml

$\frac{1}{2}$ pint = 275 ml

$\frac{3}{4}$ pint = 425 ml

1 pint = 575 ml

1$\frac{3}{4}$ pints = 1000 ml (1 litre)

3 pints = 1$\frac{1}{2}$ litres

CONTENTS

© D C P and E J P, 1993. Reprinted 1995 (twice), 1996
Cover photograph by Jonathan Tew
Drawings by Craig Hildrew

ISBN 1 85772 057 1
Typeset by Domino Books (Wales) Ltd

The following charts give the approximate equivalents for metric and imperial weights, and oven temperatures.

Ounces	Approx g to nearest whole number	Approx g to nearest whole 25 g
1	28	25
2	57	50
3	85	75
4	113	125
5	142	150
6	170	175
7	198	200
8	226	225
9	255	250
10	283	275
11	311	300
12	340	350
13	368	375
14	396	400
15	428	425
16	456	450

OVEN TEMPERATURE GUIDE

	Electricity		Gas Mark
	°C	°F	
Very cool	110	225	¼
	130	250	½
Cool	140	275	1
	150	300	2
Moderate	170	325	3
	180	350	4
Moderately hot	190	375	5
	200	400	6
Hot	220	425	7
	230	450	8
Very hot	240	475	9

When using this chart for weights over 16 ounces, add the appropriate figures in the column giving the nearest whole number of grammes and then adjust to the nearest unit of 25. For example, 18 oz (16 oz + 2 oz) becomes 456 + 57 = 513 to the nearest whole number and 525 g to the nearest unit of 25.

A CUP OF TEA

Tea is a drink for all occasions and all people. It warms, calms and soothes. The British drink more tea per head than any other nation and at times of crisis, the cry is 'put the kettle on,' the first stage in the ritual of making a *cuppa*.

The origins of tea drinking lie in myths. One legend relates that more than 5,000 years ago the Chinese Emperor, Shên Nûng, the Divine Cultivator, while wandering round his Empire sheltered under a tree to boil his drinking water. Some leaves from a nearby bush fell into the water and he liked the resulting brew so much that he started to grow the plant for himself. This may have been the first cup of tea. The Japanese adopted the drink in the eighth century and an intricate tea ceremony evolved. The commodity was first brought to Europe from China and Japan by the Dutch in 1610. At first it was regarded as an expensive novelty and was a short-lived craze in France. The East India Company, under its charter granted by Elizabeth I, recorded ships reaching China in 1637 but tea did not feature in their records until 1644.

Tea first made its way into the new and fashionable coffee houses. Thomas Garway of Garraways Coffee House, Exchange Alley, Cornhill, London was one of the first to see the potential of selling it and his first public sale took place in 1657. In 1660, he issued a broadsheet offering tea for sale at £6 to £10 per pound. He claimed it was *wholesome, preserving perfect health until extreme old age, good for clearing the sight . . .* and that it was a panacea for a range of ailments, curing *gripping of the guts, colds, dropsies, scurveys and it could make the body active and lusty.*

The first advertisement for the beverage appeared in the newspaper, *Mercurius Politicus,* on September 30, 1658. The owner of The Sultaness Head Coffee House offered *China Tcha, Tay* or *Tee.* By 1700 there were more than 500 coffee houses in London selling it. Samuel Pepys, the diarist, liked the new drink and on Sunday, September 25, 1660 first tried *a cup of tee (a China drink) of which I never drank before.* Inn keepers were not pleased as people took up tea drinking at the coffee houses and the Government was concerned about the drop in revenue from taxes as the sale of wines and liquor fell. Charles II suggested that coffee houses were nothing more than centres of sedition and intrigue. In a proclamation in 1675 he forbade the sale of coffee, chocolate, sherbet and tea from people's homes and made it illegal to keep a public coffee house. This aroused widespread ill feeling and resentment and wisely the law was not enforced. However, an Act in 1676 attempted to control coffee houses by requiring anyone wishing to open one to obtain a licence at the Quarter Sessions. The Act also tried to impose duty on all liquor sold at such houses but it proved impossible to enforce.

In 1664, the East India Company made Charles II a present of tea. In 1689 it began to import tea direct from China and in 1721 it was given a monopoly of the trade in this commodity that lasted until 1833. The Company was wound up in 1834 mainly because of the expansion of the new Indian Empire: people felt that the Company was keeping the price too high.

Drinking tea has had a remarkable effect on the culture and lifestyle of the British. (It has even been important in the loss of a colony)* Queen Catherine, wife of Charles II, brought chests of tea to Britain as part of her wedding dowry and introduced the habit of drinking it socially, a custom continued by the royal family today.

The tradition of the *tea lady* began with a Mrs Harries, wife of the Housekeeper and Beadle of the East India Company. When she made tea for the Committee Meetings held by the Directors of the Company in 1666 she began a line of ladies reknown for their cheerfulness and reliability. Tea breaks have been the traditional right of workers for over 200 years. At one time such breaks were considered a waste of time but now it is realised that a short break actually increases the efficiency of the workforce. In recent years there has been a tendency to replace the tea lady with a vending machine but the drink produced does not taste as good.

*In 1760 few Americans except a small band of extremists dreamed of breaking ties with England. However, in 1768 while the colonists were rejoicing at the repeal of the hated Stamp Act, the British Chancellor of the Exchequer attempted to raise money by levying customs duties on glass, lead, paint, paper and tea imported into America. There were widespread protests and the British government relented but the tax on tea was left as a token of the British parliament's right to impose such duties. Resentment against British rule from afar smouldered. In 1773 it was decreed that the East India Company should ship tea direct to the colonies. This meant American ships could no longer carry this commodity between England and America. This loss of revenue united American agitators and merchants and it was declared that no more tea should be landed at Boston. On 16 December, 1773, $75,000 worth of tea was flung into the harbour. The response by the British government to this 'Boston Tea Party', as it came to be called, was the next step along the path to the American colonies achieving independence and the birth of the USA.

AFTERNOON TEA

Tea came to be regarded as a suitable beverage for the whole family, especially the ladies of the house. A special tray contained all the paraphernalia needed for the hostess to make the tea in front of her family or guests. When a cup was empty, she would refill it until the guests remembered to put their spoons inside the cups. (Today, it is the custom for hotels to prepare a similar tray in each bedroom - a much appreciated welcome.) Tea gardens with family entertainment sprang up all around London and the major towns. The entertainment included dancing and this evolved into the Tea Dance which remained a fashionable pastime until the Second World War (1939 - 45).

The custom of taking afternoon tea is thought to have been started by Anna, 7th. Duchess of Bedford in the early 1800s because she felt hungry between lunch and dinner. At about the same time, the Earl of Sandwich thought of putting a filling between two slices of bread. The sandwich and a cuppa made a perfect afternoon snack, a time for meeting friends at the end of the day and before the exertions of the night's entertainment: teatime. Governesses turned this into the nursery tea, usually a more substantial meal. For the working classes, afternoon tea became high tea. This was somewhere between the delicate offerings of the drawing room and the generous courses of the dinners of the gentry and it became the main evening meal for the working classes.

Tea shops were the idea of a manageress of the Aerated Bread Company, the first shop opened in 1864 and the idea spread rapidly. Such shops and Lyons Corner Houses became one of the few places where an unchaperoned lady could meet friends without damaging her reputation. As the pace of life has quickened, most such leisurely establishments have given way to fast food and take-away outlets. Nevertheless, afternoon tea remains one of the more civilised traditions that can still be enjoyed.

Afternoon Tea
Assorted Sandwiches
Scones or Muffins
Cream Cakes
Pastries
Biscuits
Tea
Milk or Slices of Lemon
Sugar

c. 1755

Cream Tea
Scones
Strawberry Jam
Clotted Cream
Tea
Slices of Lemon or Milk
Sugar

TYPES OF TEA

There was always extensive betting on the Tea Races of the 1860s. The opening of the Suez Canal in 1869 and the introduction of steam power ended this romantic element of the trade.

Prices were high and governments saw an easy way to raise revenue from taxes on imported tea and a thriving black market grew based on smuggling. Traditionally, clergymen on the coast hired out their crypts as warehouses for illicit tea.

Tea is an important source of income for a government: from the taxes paid by growers and buyers and as a source of foreign exchange. Britain imports the commodity from the subcontinents of India, Sri Lanka (formerly Ceylon), Indonesia and East Africa and a little from China, the birthplace of tea. It has been cultivated in **China** for more than 1500 years and China dominated the trade until the 1850s. She is still a major producer but is best known for her speciality blends such as Keemun, Lapsang, Souchong, Oolongs and green tea. **India** produces some 30% of the world's total. The British first planted tea in India in the 1850s near Assam. Three areas are important: Assam produces strong mature black varieties which are blended to yield a beverage that is ideal for drinking with milk; Darjeeling in the foothills of the Himalayas produces India's most prized varieties. Grown at altitudes of up to 6,500 feet, the bushes may take ten years to mature and this tea is expensive. Nilgiri, a high plateau in the south of India yields those with a taste between the mature Assams and the sharper ones of Sri Lanka and are used extensively in blending. **Sri Lanka** is the world's third largest producer and second largest exporter. Ceylon as it then was suffered coffee blight and replaced its coffee plantations by tea in the 1870s. There was competition between the carriers and in 1849 the laws banning American ships from competing on the China to England run were repealed. The sleek New England clippers were faster than the older Aberdeen-built ships by as much as four days. There was always extensive betting on the Tea Races of the 1860s. The opening of the Suez Canal in 1869 and the introduction of steam power ended this romantic element of the trade.

The tea bush, an evergreen plant, is a member of the Camellia family and probably originated in the mountain forests along the border of Burma and India with China. Growing wild, it can reach a height of 10 m (30 ft) but the cultivated plant is pruned to keep it at a height of 1.5m (5 ft). This makes it easier to pick the leaves and also encourages the growth of the leaves. The plant can be grown up to 2,200 m (7000 ft) above sea level and from the equator to latitude 45°. Heavy rainfall and an acid soil are needed and the best fields are found above 1200 m (4000 ft). The oval-shaped, shiny leaves are picked by hand. Every 7 to 14 days, the bud and 2 terminal leaves are removed from each shoot. An experienced picker can gather up to 27/33 kg (60/70 lb) a day. In warmer climates, for example in Sri Lanka, a bush produces tea in its fourth year and can be harvested all year. At higher altitudes or in cooler areas, plants may take up to 10 years to mature and are plucked only in the growing season. A bush can last for some 50 years.

There are three kinds of tea - green, oolong and black with black making up about 98% of all exports to the West; the various kinds are produced from the same bushes by treating the leaves in different ways.

The Main Stages in the Tea Process
Withering For up to 24 hours hot air is passed over the freshly plucked leaves spread out on trays. Up to 40% of their weight is lost.
Rolling This breaks up the leaves releasing essential oils and enzymes.
Sieving Vibrating sieves separate the finer leaves from the coarser material which is rolled and sieved again.
Fermenting This involves oxidation in a humid atmosphere and usually takes about four hours. The tea becomes brown in colour. Green tea, a favourite in China, is not fermented and oolong is fermented for a very short time.
Firing Fermentation is stopped by passing very hot air over the tea which is then packed for storage and transportation.

Grading Teas are graded as leaf or broken. Grading does not indicate quality but

When tea first became popular it was so expensive caddies were kept locked. There were usually two: one for the black and one for the green leaf.
Tea sets too were in demand. Often they had two teapots, the second may have been for coffee. There was also difficulty in producing enough cups and saucers and plates with the same pattern. Shopkeepers complained of 'false packing' when they opened their orders and found that patterns failed to match.

c. 1815

In Victorian times, there were books full of advice on etiquette and warnings on how not to do it. Gentlemen drank from moustache cups in which there was a small ledge inside the brim: a moustache rested on this without getting wet.
For the Edwardians, the accepted time for tea was 5 o'clock. Sometimes the occasion was more like high tea with footmen handing round the cups and hot dishes on the menu.

the size and appearance of the leaves. Broken teas are graded Broken Orange Pekoe, Broken Pekoe, Broken Pekoe Souchong, Fannings and Dust. Leaf teas are graded Orange Pekoe, Pekoe and Souchong. Tippy or Flower Grades apply to Darjeelings only: they are large leafed, contain a high proportion of buds and are picked at the beginning of the season. In 1979 the Tea Council launched the Catering Tea Grading Scheme which established three independent standards indicated by a star rating.

Trading takes place traditionally in London and Amsterdam and also in the producer countries. Samples are made up and examined and tasted.

Blending Almost all black tea is blended to give the required taste and colour. Once retailers made up different blends to suit individual customers and packed them in home-made bags at the shop counter.

Packaging Loose tea should be kept in an air-tight, light-proof container at room temperature. Adulteration was once a major problem. John Horniman was the first to sell the commodity in sealed packages bearing his name as a guarantee of quality. Tea bags may date from 1904 when an American tea merchant, Thomas Sullivan, sent samples in little silk bags but they did not become popular in the UK until the 1950s. On the routes to Russia and Tibet, tea was made into compressed tablets and shavings from these were boiled with water.

WAYS OF DRINKING TEA

Green tea has been drunk in **Japan** since the eighth or ninth century. It came to be associated with the rise of Zen Buddhism as monks considered it calmed the mind. They adopted the drink as part of their ceremonial life. Traditionally, the tea ceremony took place in a house specially built in a secluded part of the garden.

First a light meal is served, then after a break, the ceremony begins with the drinking of a thick liquor made from powdered green tea. Finally, a thin beverage is served. **The West** originally drank the green variety but after 1660 those drunk with milk became more popular. **America** rejected milk and eventually achieved independence by introducing iced tea. In **Australia,** the 'billy' can is used to boil water in the outback - it is also used to make stews. **Morocco** is the only country outside the Far East where green tea is widely drunk (with sugar and spearmint leaves). **Russians** use a samovar, a water heater on top of which is a small teapot containing very strong tea essence. A little of the essence is placed in small glasses and topped up with water from the samovar. In **Tibet,** chips from a tea brick are put in cold water and boiled for hours. Salt and rancid yak butter are added before the beverage is served in small wooden bowls.

EXOTIC TEAS

For centuries, the Chinese have produced scented teas using flowers, fruits and oils. These are best drunk without milk. Spiced, they make warming winter drinks and fruit varieties are delicious iced. Earl Grey is based on an original recipe given to the second Earl Grey in 1850 by a Chinese mandarin. It is a blend of fine black teas flavoured with the oil of the bergamot orange.

TISANES are herb teas drunk as medicines and for refreshment. They are made from flowers or leaves in the pot in the usual way but may need to be boiled for up to 5 minutes. Their efficacy is traditional. Rose petals produce a sharp tasting drink, elderflower is a mild stimulant, chrysanthemum is a popular Chinese drink, orange blossom is used as a treatment for stomach problems and ulcers, rosehip is rich in vitamin C, fennel is good for raised blood pressure, lime blossom is used as a treatment for headaches, lemon verbena reduces fever, raspberry leaf eases childbirth, thyme and cinnamon are good for colds and nettle eases rheumatic pain.

Tea drinking improved the nation's health. Water had to be boiled and it replaced gin.
The teapot with two spouts enabled tea of different strengths to be poured from the one pot. The earliest teapots, made at Yi-Hsing near Shanghai, came over with the first tea. From 1760 Josiah Wedgwood led the mass production of earthenware and set the seal on the style of the English teapot. His wife tested every design for its pouring qualities and strength. In 1800 Josiah Spode first made English porcelain.

TO MAKE TEA

Warm the pot, add a teaspoon of tea (or tea bag) for each person plus one for the pot and pour on boiling water. Leave to stand for five minutes and then serve with slices of lemon or milk.

If served with milk, always pour the milk into the cup first.

ICED TEA

This can be made quickly by pouring hot tea over iced cubes. It is served alone or with slices of lemon.

Alternatively, steep 50 g (2 oz) of tea in 1 litre (2 pints) of cold water for three hours or overnight. To serve, strain over ice cubes in a glass.

Planter's Tea

2 pints strong tea	*¼ pint lemon juice*
1 pint dark rum	*brown sugar*
¼ pint orange juice	*lemon slices*

Mix the liquids together and heat until hot but not boiling. Add soft brown sugar to taste. Serve hot, decorated with lemon slices.

Spiced Tea Punch

1 pint hot tea	*stick of cinnamon*
1 pint red wine	*4 cloves*
2 tablespoons brandy	*½ lemon (sliced)*
1 tablespoon caster sugar	

Put all the ingredients except the brandy and sugar into a saucepan and bring to the boil. Simmer for five minutes. Stir in the sugar. Remove from the heat and add the brandy. Pour into a punch bowl.

Rum Cup

1 pint iced tea	*¼ pint orange juice*
½ pint lemonade	*sugar*
¼ pint dark rum	*orange slices*

Mix the liquids together. Add sugar to taste. Pour into glasses and serve decorated with orange slices.

CAKES

RICH CHOCOLATE CAKE

METRIC
Cake
150 g butter
150 g caster sugar
3 eggs
150 g self raising four
25 g cocoa
Chocolate Butter Icing
200 g butter
300 g icing sugar
6 tablespoons cocoa
8 tablespoons boiling water

IMPERIAL
Cake
6 oz butter
6 oz caster sugar
3 eggs
6 oz self raising flour
1 oz cocoa
Chocolate Butter Icing
8 oz butter
12 oz icing sugar
6 tablespoons cocoa
8 tablespoons boiling water

Chocolate Cake Grease two 17.5 cm (7 in) sandwich cake tins and line with greased greaseproof paper. Cream the butter and sugar until fluffy. Beat the eggs into the mixture one at a time, adding a teaspoon of flour. Sift the flour and cocoa together and fold into the mixture. If using an electric mixture, do not over beat at this stage. (Or fold in by hand using a metal spoon.) Add a little milk if the mixture seems dry. Divide the mixture between the two tins and smooth the surface. Bake in a moderately hot oven (190°C, 375°F, gas mark 5) for 25 minutes until the cake springs back when pressed lightly. Turn on to a wire tray to cool. Sandwich together with butter icing.

Chocolate Butter Icing Cream the butter and icing sugar together. Dissolve the cocoa in the boiling water. Allow to cool a little then beat into the creamed mixture. Use half the icing to sandwich the cakes together and the remainder to decorate the tops and sides. Decorate with chocolate buttons or triangles or chocolate strands.

STRAWBERRY CREAM GATEAU

METRIC
Sponge
4 eggs
150 g caster sugar
100 g plain flour
pinch of salt
Filling
6 tablespoons strawberry jam
100 g low fat cheese
3 tablespoons cream
1 tablespoon icing sgar
strawberries

IMPERIAL
Sponge
4 eggs
6 oz caster sugar
4 oz plain flour
pinch of salt
Filling
6 tablespoons strawberry jam
4 oz low fat cheese
3 tablespoons cream
1 tablespoon icing sugar
strawberries

Grease a 20 cm (8 in) cake tin. Beat the eggs and caster sugar together using an electric beater until the beaters leave a trail that lasts a few seconds. Sift the flour and salt together and then fold into the beaten mixture. Turn the sponge mixture into the tin. Bake in a moderately hot oven (190°C, 375°F, gas mark 5) for 20 - 25 minutes until the cake springs back when lightly pressed. Turn on to a wire rack and leave to cool. Cut the cake into two halves and spread each half with strawberry jam. Whip cheese, cream and icing sugar together and use one third of the mixture to sandwich the pieces of cake together. Spread the remaining mixture over the top and sides. Decorate with strawberries. Keep chilled until served.

PEACHES AND CREAM GATEAU

Follow the recipe above for Strawberry Cream Gateau but replace the strawberry jam by apricot jam and decorate with peach halves or slices.

LEMON CREAM GATEAU

Follow the recipe above for Strawberry Cream Gateau and fold the grated rind and juice of a lemon into the mixture with the flour. Replace the strawberry jam by lemon curd and decorate with crystallised lemon slices.

DUNDEE CAKE

METRIC	IMPERIAL
100 g currants	4 oz currants
100 g seedless raisins	4 oz seedless raisins
50 g chopped, blanched almonds	2 oz chopped, blanched almonds
100 g chopped mixed peel	4 oz chopped mixed peel
1 lemon	1 lemon
250 g plain flour	10 oz plain flour
200 g butter	8 oz butter
200 g brown sugar	8 oz brown sugar
4 eggs	4 eggs
25 g split almonds	1 oz split almonds

Grease a 20 cm (8 in) round cake tin and line with greased greaseproof paper. Mix the fruit, mixed peel and chopped almonds together in a bowl. Grate the rind of the lemon. Cream the butter and sugar until light and fluffy and beat in the grated lemon rind. Add the eggs, one at a time, to the creamed mixture. Beat well after each addition. Sift the flour and fold into the creamed mixture. Fold in the fruit and nut mix. Turn the cake mixture into the tin. Make a slight dip in the centre and arrange the split almonds around the top of the cake. Bake in a moderate oven (170ºC, 325ºF, gas mark 3) for two and a half hours until cooked. (A clean knife inserted into the cake should not show any trace of moist cake when withdrawn.)

MADEIRA CAKE

METRIC	IMPERIAL
100 g plain flour	4 oz plain flour
100 g self raising flour	4 oz self raising flour
150 g butter	6 oz butter
150 g caster sugar	6 oz caster sugar
1 teaspoon vanilla flavouring	1 teaspoon vanilla flavouring
3 eggs	3 eggs
1 tablespoon milk	1 tablespoon milk
3 slices of citron peel	3 slices of citron peel

Grease an 17.5 cm (7 inch) round cake tin and line with greased greaseproof paper. Sift the flours together. Cream the butter and sugar together until pale and fluffy. Beat in the vanilla essence. Beat in the eggs, one at a time. Fold in the flour using a metal spoon. Add a little milk if necessary to give a dropping consistency. Turn the mixture into the tin and bake in a moderate oven (180ºC, 350ºF, gas mark 4) for 1 - 1½ hours. After 20 minutes, place the citron peel slices on top of the cake and continue baking until the cake is firm. Turn on to a wire tray to cool.

ORANGE MADEIRA CAKE

Add the grated orange rind of 2 oranges to the creamed butter and sugar mixture.

SEED CAKE

Using the recipe for Madeira Cake above, stir 2 teaspoons of caraway seeds into the flour. Omit the slices of citron peel.

(In Victorian times, Madeira cake was traditionally served with a glass of Madeira wine.)

VICTORIA SANDWICH

METRIC
150 g butter
150 g caster sugar
150 g self raising flour
3 eggs
jam

IMPERIAL
6 oz butter
6 oz caster sugar
6 oz self raising flour
3 eggs
jam

Grease two 20 cm (8 in) sandwich tins and line with greased greaseproof paper. Cream the butter and sugar together until light and fluffy. Beat the eggs and beat into the creamed mixture. Sift the flour and fold into the creamed mixture using a metal spoon. Divide the mixture equally between the two tins and level the tops. Bake in a hot oven (190ºC, 375ºF, gas mark 5) for 20 minutes until the cake springs back when lightly pressed. Place on a wire tray to cool. Sandwich the cakes together with jam and dust with caster sugar.

ICED CAKES

Make the cake mixture as in the recipe for Victoria Sandwich above but use rectangular cake tins instead of round ones. Cut the cooked, cooled cake into squares and cover each with different coloured glacé icing. Before the icing hardens decorate with some of the following: chocolate buttons, hundreds and thousands, desiccated coconut, chocolate flakes, glacé cherries, orange and lemon slices, chocolate triangles or strawberries.

ENGLISH MADELEINES

Make the cake mixture as in the recipe above but bake in madeleine moulds or muffin tins. When cooked and cooled, cut off the bottoms so that the cakes stand upright. Coat with red jam (sieved and melted) and desiccated coconut.

CHOCOLATE BUTTON CAKES

Make the cake mixture as in the recipe for Victoria Sandwich but replace 2 tablespoons of the flour by 2 tablespoons cocoa. Sift the flour and cocoa together. Bake the cake mixture in paper cases in patty tins in a hot oven (190°C, 375°F, gas mark 5) for 10 - 15 minutes. Decorate with glacé icing and chocolate buttons.

Glacé icing: Add 1 tablespoon warm water and a few drops of vanilla flavouring to 100 g (4 oz) sifted icing sugar in a bowl. Stir until the mixture is smooth and coats the back of a spoon.

Chocolate glacé icing: Dissolve 2 teaspoons cocoa in the warm water before it is added to the icing sugar.

FRUIT CAKES

METRIC	IMPERIAL
200 g plain flour	8 oz plain flour
2 teaspoons baking powder	2 teaspoons baking powder
1 teaspoon mixed spice	1 teaspoon mixed spice
100 g butter	4 oz butter
rind of 1 lemon (grated)	rind of 1 lemon (grated)
100 g demerara sugar	4 oz demerara sugar
100 g mixed dried fruit	4 oz mixed dried fruit
1 egg	1 egg
2 teaspoons milk	2 teaspoons milk

Grease two baking sheets. Sift the flour, baking powder and mixed spice together. Rub in the butter until the mixture looks like breadcrumbs. Stir in the grated lemon rind, sugar and fruit. Lightly beat the egg. Make a well in the middle of the cake mixture and pour in the egg. Add a little milk if necessary to bind the mixture to give a stiff crumbly texture. Divide the mixture into rough heaps and bake in a moderately hot oven (200°C, 400°F, gas mark 6) for 15 - 20 minutes.

SCONES
AFTERNOON TEA SCONES

METRIC	IMPERIAL
200 g self raising flour	*8 oz self raising flour*
1 teaspoon baking powder	*1 teaspoon baking powder*
pinch of salt	*pinch of salt*
2 tablespoons caster sugar	*2 tablespoons caster sugar*
50 g butter	*2 oz butter*
1 egg	*1 egg*
5 tablespoons milk	*5 tablespoons milk*

Sift the flour, baking powder and salt together. Stir in the sugar. Rub in the butter until the mixture looks like breadcrumbs. Lightly beat the egg with the milk. Make a well in the centre of the flour mixture and add the egg and milk. Mix to a firm dough. Turn on to a floured board and knead lightly until the dough is smooth. Lightly roll out to a thickness of 2 cm (¾ in) and cut into 4 cm (1½ in) rounds. Brush with milk and place on the baking tray. Bake in a hot oven (230°C, 450°F, gas mark 8) for 10 - 15 minutes until golden. To keep scones soft, wrap in a tea cloth. For crusty scones, cool on a wire tray. Serve warm, buttered or with jam and cream (clotted if possible).

FRUIT SCONES

Use the recipe for Afternoon Tea Scones. After rubbing in the butter, stir in 50 g (2 oz) mixed dried fruit.

CHEESE SCONES

Use the recipe for Afternoon Tea Scones but use 40 g (1½ oz) butter instead of 50 g (2 oz). After rubbing in the butter, stir in 50 g (2 oz) grated Cheddar cheese. After brushing the scones with milk, sprinkle the tops with a little more grated cheese and bake in a hot oven (220°C, 4250°F, gas mark 8) for 10 minutes.

GRIDDLE SCONES

Make the scone mixture as in the recipes for Afternoon Tea Scones or Fruit Scones but cook on a lightly greased griddle or thick frying pan. Turn the scones after a few minutes to cook both sides.

HONEY SCONES

METRIC	IMPERIAL
200 g plain flour	8 oz plain flour
3 teaspoons baking powder	3 teaspoons baking powder
1 teaspoon mixed spice	1 teaspoon mixed spice
pinch of salt	pinch of salt
50 g butter	2 oz butter
3 teaspoons caster sugar	3 teaspoons caster sugar
75 g chopped walnuts	3 oz chopped walnuts
2 teaspoons lemon juice	2 teaspoons lemon juice
150 ml milk	¼ pint milk
honey	honey

Sift the flour, baking powder, mixed spice and salt together. Rub in the butter until the mixture looks like breadcrumbs. Stir in the sugar and two thirds of the walnuts. Stir the lemon juice into the milk and add to the scone mixture. Turn on to a floured board and knead lightly until the dough is smooth. Lightly roll out to a square (about 20 cm - 8 in square). Mark into 5 cm (2 in) squares. Brush with milk and sprinkle the rest of the chopped walnuts over the dough. Bake in a hot oven (220ºC, 425ºF, gas mark 7) for 15 - 20 minutes until firm. Cut into the marked squares and brush with honey. Delicious served warm.

FRUIT LOAVES AND BUNS

TEABREAD

METRIC	IMPERIAL
150 g raisins	6 oz raisins
150 g sultanas	6 oz sultanas
50 g currants	2 oz currants
300 ml strained tea	½ pint strained tea
150 g brown sugar	6 oz brown sugar
1 egg	1 egg
200 g wholemeal flour	8 oz wholemeal flour
½ teaspoon baking powder	½ teaspoon baking powder
½ teaspoon ground mixed spice	½ teaspoon ground mixed spice

Soak the fruit and sugar in the tea overnight. Sift the flour, baking powder and mixed spice together. Lightly beat the egg. Add the flour mixture and egg to the fruit and tea. Beat thoroughly until well mixed. Grease and line an 800 g (2 lb) loaf tin with greased greaseproof paper. Turn the mixture into the tin and bake in a moderate oven (180°C, 350°F, gas mark 4) for 1½ hours until the teabread is well risen and a clean knife inserted into it has no trace of the mixture when withdrawn. Turn on to a wire rack to cool. Store in an airtight container for a day or two before serving sliced and buttered. It is also delicious toasted.

CURRANT BUN

METRIC
75 g butter
100 g caster sugar
2 eggs
75 g currants
pinch ground nutmeg
200 g plain flour
1 teaspoon baking powder
pinch of salt
2 tablespoons millk

IMPERIAL
3 oz butter
4 oz caster sugar
2 eggs
3 oz currants
pinch ground nutmeg
8 oz plain flour
1 teaspoon baking powder
pinch of salt
2 tablespoons milk

Grease and line a 20 cm (8 in) sandwich tin with greased greaseproof paper. Cream the butter and sugar together until light and fluffy. Beat the eggs and add to the creamed mixture. Sift the flour, baking powder, salt and nutmeg together and stir into the butter mixture. Stir in the fruit. Add the milk to make a fairly stiff dough. Turn the mixture into the tin and bake in a moderate oven (180°C, 350°F, gas mark 4) for 1 hour until the bun is well risen. Serve sliced and buttered or toasted.

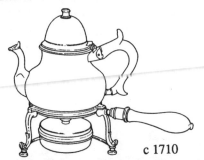

c 1710

TEACAKES

METRIC
400 g plain flour
pinch of salt
25 g butter
15 g fresh yeast or
  7 g dried yeast and 1 teaspoon caster sugar
200 ml tepid milk
75 g mixed dried fruit
Glaze
1 teaspoon caster sugar
2 tablespoons milk

IMPERIAL
1 lb plain flour
pinch of salt
1 oz butter
½ oz fresh yeast or
  ¼ oz dried yeast and 1 teaspoon caster sugar
⅓ pint tepid milk
3 oz mixed dried fruit
Glaze
1 teaspoon caster sugar
2 tablespoons milk

Sift the flour and salt into a bowl. Cream the yeast with the sugar and a little of the tepid milk. Cover with a cloth and leave to stand for 15 minutes until frothy. (If dried yeast is used, dissolve the teaspoon of sugar in all the tepid milk and stir in the dried yeast. Leave to stand in a warm place for 15 minutes until frothy.) Make a well in the centre of the flour and add the yeast and milk to form a soft elastic dough. Knead for ten minutes until the dough is smooth. Work in the fruit. Cover with a cloth and leave in a warm place for an hour or so until the dough has doubled in size. Divide into six pieces. Knead each piece and flatten with the palm of the hand into a round of diameter 10 cm (4 in). Place the rounds on two greased baking sheets. Prick the surface of the cakes with a fork. Cover and leave to rise for 15 minutes. Bake in a moderately hot oven (200°C, 400°F, gas mark 6) for 15 - 20 minutes.
Glaze Dissolve the sugar in the milk. When the teacakes have cooked and are still very hot, brush the tops with the glaze to make them shine. Serve hot, split and buttered or toasted.

PASTRIES

APPLE PIE

METRIC	IMPERIAL
Shortcrust pastry	*Shortcrust pastry*
200 g plain flour	*8 oz plain flour*
100 g butter	*4 oz butter*
8 teaspoons cold water	*8 teaspoons cold water*
pinch of salt	*pinch of salt*
Filling	*Filling*
1 kilo cooking apples	*2 lb cooking apples*
sugar	*sugar*

Filling Peel, core and slice the apples. Cover with water in a saucepan and bring to the boil to soften the fruit. Add sugar to taste.

Pastry Sift the flour and salt together. Rub in the butter until the mixture looks like breadcrumbs. Add the water and form the pastry into a lump. Roll out half the pastry on a floured board and use to line a 25 cm (10 in) ovenproof plate. Spread the apples over the pastry with as much juice as possible. Roll out the rest of the pastry and cover the apples. Brush with milk and sprinkle lightly with sugar. Bake in a moderately hot oven (200°C, 400°F, gas mark 6) for 20 minutes until the pastry is cooked and lightly browned. Serve with whipped cream or ice cream.

BLACKBERRY AND APPLE PIE

Using the recipe for Apple Pie, replace half the weight of the apples by blackberries and cook as above.

STRAWBERRY AND CREAM BUNS

METRIC	IMPERIAL
65 g plain flour	2¼ oz plain flour
pinch of salt	pinch of salt
50 g butter	2 oz butter
2 eggs	2 eggs
125 ml water	¼ pint water
400 g strawberries	1 lb strawberries
25 g sugar	1 oz sugar
125 ml double cream	¼ pint double cream

Sift the flour and salt. Slowly heat the butter in the water in a saucepan until the butter has melted. Heat strongly until the mixture boils. Lower the heat and add the flour and salt. Stir and work into a soft ball that leaves the sides of the saucepan. Remove from the heat and allow to cool a little. Add the eggs one at a time, beating until the mixture is smooth and shiny. Pipe or spoon buns on to a greased baking sheet and bake in a moderately hot oven (200°C, 400°F, gas mark 6) for 10 minutes until the pastry is cooked and lightly browned. Remove from the oven and cut a small opening in each. Return to the oven for a further five minutes. Cool on a wire tray. Wash and hull the strawberries. Whip the cream. Fill the buns with strawberries and cream.

APPLE AND CREAM BUNS

Make buns as in the recipe for Strawberry Cream Buns above. Peel, core and slice 400 g (1 lb) cooking apples. Cover with water and heat gently until the fruit is soft. Add sugar to taste. Fill the buns with the apples and whipped cream.

APPLE MERINGUE FLAN

METRIC
Flan case
100 g plain flour
pinch of salt
75 g butter
1 teaspoon caster sugar
1 egg (beaten)
Filling
400 g cooking apples
sugar
1 tablespoon sieved apricot jam
Meringue
2 egg-whites
100 g caster sugar

IMPERIAL
Flan case
4 oz plain flour
pinch of salt
3 oz butter
1 teaspoon caster sugar
1 egg (beaten)
Filling
1 lb cooking apples
sugar
1 tablespoon sieved apricot jam
Meringue
2 egg-whites
4 oz caster sugar

Flan case Sift the flour and salt together. Rub the butter into the flour until the mixture looks like breadcrumbs. Stir in the sugar. Add the egg and stir with a knife until the ingredients begin to stick together. With one hand, draw the mixture together and knead lightly for a few seconds until the dough is smooth. Turn on to a floured board and roll out and use to line a 17.5 cm (7 in) flan case. Bake blind so that the pastry will remain flat. [To bake blind, line the flan tin with the pastry and chill in the refrigerator for 30 minutes. Prick the bottom base of the pastry all over with a fork. Cut a piece of foil or greaseproof paper to fit the base of the pastry case. Crumple it to make it fit easily and use to line the pastry case. Cover the base with rice, or crusts of bread or ceramic beans. Bake in a moderately hot oven (200°C, 400°F, gas mark 6) for 10 - 15 minutes until the pastry is set. Remove the foil or paper and rice, crusts or beans and cook for a further 5 minutes until the pastry is firm and golden brown. Leave to cool.]

Filling Peel, core and slice the apples. Cover with water in a saucepan and bring to the boil to soften the fruit. Add sugar to taste. Cover the base of the flan case with the jam to prevent moisture soaking in. Spoon the fruit into the

flan case.
Meringue Whisk the egg-whites until they form peaks. Whisk in half the sugar until the meringue is shiny. Fold in the remaining sugar using a metal spoon. Spread over the fruit making sure that the meringue touches the edge of the flan case. Place in a cool oven (150°C, 300°F, gas mark 2) for 20 minutes to set the meringue.

STRAWBERRY TARTS

Flan cases Make the pastry as on page 26. Cut into 7.5 cm (3 in) circles using a fluted pastry cutter and use to line individual flan tins or 24 deep patty tins. Bake blind.
Filling Warm 300 g (12 oz) apricot jam with 2 tablespoons lemon juice. Sieve. Brush the base of the pastry cases with the jam mixture. Wash and hull 400 g (1 lb) strawberries and arrange in the pastry cases. Brush the fruit with the remaining jam mixture as glaze. Decorate with whipped cream.

MINI LEMON CHEESECAKES

METRIC
Pastry cases
Filling
200 g full fat soft cheese
2 eggs (beaten)
25 g caster sugar
2 teaspoons plain flour
juice and grated rind of ½ a lemon

IMPERIAL
Pastry cases
Filling
8 oz full fat soft cheese
2 eggs (beaten)
1 oz caster sugar
2 teaspoons plain flour
juice and grated rind of ½ a lemon

Make the pastry cases as in the recipe for Strawberry Tarts. Mix all the ingredients for the filling together and beat until smooth. Pour the filling into the pastry cases and bake in a cool oven (150°C, 300°F, gas mark 2) for 15 minutes until the fillings are set. Cool on a wire rack for 30 minutes and then in a refrigerator for 1 hour. Before serving decorate with lemon slices, crumbled chocolate flakes or whipped cream.

TRIFLES AND CREAMS

SHERRY TRIFLE

METRIC
Trifle
8 sponge cakes
100 g macaroons
strawberry jam
200 ml sherry
250 ml cream
toasted, flaked almonds
Custard
500 ml milk
⅟ vanilla pod
2 eggs and 2 egg yolks
2 tablespoons caster sugar

IMPERIAL
Trifle
8 sponge cakes
4 oz macaroons
strawberry jam
⅟ pint sherry
⅟ pint cream
toasted, flaked almonds
Custard
1 pint milk
⅟ vanilla pod
2 eggs and 2 egg yolks
2 tablespoons caster sugar

Trifle Split and jam the sponge cakes and place at the bottom of a glass trifle dish. Place the macaroons on top of the sponge cakes. Pour the sherry over the cakes and macaroons and leave to stand for 30 minutes. Pour on the cooled custard and decorate with whipped cream and toasted, flaked almonds.

Custard Warm the milk with the vanilla pod until just boiling. Remove from the heat and leave to stand for 20 minutes. Remove the pod. Beat the eggs, egg yolks and sugar together and stir into the milk. Warm gently, stirring until the custard thickens slightly. Do not allow to boil. Sprinkle a little sugar over the surface or cover the saucepan with a damp cloth (to stop a skin forming) and leave to cool. (If you do not have a vanilla pod, add a few drops of vanilla essence to the milk.)

STRAWBERRY SYLLABUB TRIFLES

METRIC	IMPERIAL
400 g strawberries	1 lb strawberries
150 g macaroons	6 oz macaroons
3 egg whites	3 egg whites
150 g caster sugar	6 oz caster sugar
150 ml white wine	¼ pint white wine
½ a lemon	½ a lemon
2 tablespoons brandy	2 tablespoons brandy
300 ml double cream	½ pint double cream

Hull and wash the strawberries. Keep 6 back for decoration. Divide the remaining fruit and macaroons between six tall glasses or small trifle dishes placing alternate layers of strawberries and macaroons. Beat the egg whites until they are stiff, then beat in half the sugar. Fold in the rest of the sugar using a metal spoon. Squeeze the lemon. Fold the lemon juice, white wine and brandy into the egg white mixture. Beat the cream until it holds its shape. Keep back a little for decoration. Fold the egg white mixture into the cream and pour over the fruit and macaroons. Stand in the refrigerator for 2 - 3 hours. Before serving, decorate with the strawberries and cream.

c. 1825

CHOCOLATE MOUSSE

METRIC	IMPERIAL
300 g plain chocolate	*12 oz plain chocolate*
6 eggs (separated)	*6 eggs (separated)*
2 tablespoons brandy or rum	*2 tablespoons brandy or rum*
150 ml double cream	*¼ pint double cream*
crumbled chocolate flake or chocolate curls	*crumbled chocolate flake or chocolate curls*

Break the chocolate into pieces and melt in a bowl standing over hot water. Remove from the heat and beat in the egg yolks. Whisk the egg whites until stiff and fold with the brandy into the chocolate mixture using a metal spoon. Place in six ramekin dishes or tall glasses and stand in the refrigerator for 2 - 3 hours. Whip the cream. Decorate the mousses with whipped cream and crumbled chocolate flake or chocolate curls.

CRÈME BRÛLÉE

METRIC	IMPERIAL
600 ml double cream	*1 pint double cream*
4 egg yolks	*4 egg yolks*
75 g caster sugar	*3 oz caster sugar*
1 teaspoon vanilla essence	*1 teaspoon vanilla essence*

Warm the cream in a bowl standing over hot water until the cream is just below boiling. Beat the egg yolks, 50 g (2 oz) of the caster sugar and the vanilla essence together. Stir in the cream. Pour the mixture into six ramekin dishes and place in a large tin half filled with hot water. Bake in a cool oven (150°C, 300°F, gas mark 2) for 1 hour or until set. Chill for several hours in a refrigerator. Before serving, sprinkle with the remaining sugar and place under the grill to caramelise the sugar.

CRUMPETS AND MUFFINS

CRUMPETS

METRIC
300 g strong plain flour
15 g fresh yeast or
   7 g dried yeast and 1 teaspoon caster sugar
200 ml tepid water
200 ml tepid milk
½ teaspoon bicarbonate of soda
 pinch of salt

IMPERIAL
12 oz strong plain flour
½ oz fresh yeast or
   ¼ oz dried yeast and 1 teaspoon caster sugar
⅓ pint tepid water
⅓ pint tepid milk
½ teaspoon bicarbonate of soda
 pinch of salt

Sift half the flour into a bowl. Make a well in the centre of the flour. Crumble the fresh yeast and add with the tepid water. Gradually mix in the flour and beat until smooth. Cover with a cloth and leave to stand for 15 minutes until frothy. (If dried yeast is used, dissolve the teaspoon of sugar in the tepid water and sprinkle the dried yeast on top of the liquid. Leave to stand in a warm place for 15 minutes until frothy.) Sift the remaining flour, bicarbonate of soda and salt together in a large bowl. (If dried yeast is used, then all the flour is added here.) Make a well in the centre and add the yeast mixture and milk. Blend until smooth to form a thick, pouring batter. Using a wooden spoon, beat the batter for a few minutes. Cover and leave for an hour in a warm place. Beat the batter again for two minutes. Grease and heat a griddle or thick frying pan. Pour the batter into crumpet rings on the griddle (or pour in two - tablespoon lots on to the griddle). Cook until set and holes form on the surface. Turn and cook the other side. Cool. Serve toasted and buttered.

How to Butter A Crumpet Crumpets are best eaten hot and buttered. Traditionally, crumpets are toasted on both sides, the smooth side first, the holey side last to ensure the maximum absorption of butter.

ENGLISH MUFFINS

METRIC	IMPERIAL
400 g strong plain flour	*1 lb strong plain flour*
pinch of salt	*pinch of salt*
15 g fresh yeast or	*¼ oz fresh yeast or*
7 g dried yeast and 1 teaspoon caster sugar	*¼ oz dried yeast and 1 teaspoon caster sugar*
150 ml tepid water	*¼ pint tepid water*
150 ml tepid milk	*¼ pint tepid milk*
1 egg	*1 egg*
25 g butter	*1 oz butter*

Sift the flour and salt into a bowl. Make a well in the centre of the flour. Crumble the fresh yeast and add with the tepid water and milk. Gradually mix in the flour and beat until smooth. Cover with a cloth and leave to stand for 15 minutes until frothy. (If dried yeast is used, dissolve the teaspoon of sugar in the tepid water and sprinkle the dried yeast on top of the liquid. Leave to stand in a warm place for 15 minutes until frothy before adding with the milk to the flour.) Beat the egg, melt the butter and add to the mixture. Mix until a sticky dough is formed. Turn on to a floured board and knead for five minutes until smooth. Cover and leave in a warm place for an hour until the dough has doubled in size. Turn on to the floured board again and knead for about five minutes until the dough is smooth. Roll out to a thickness of 1 cm (½ in). Cut into 7.5 cm (3 in) rounds and place on two lightly floured baking sheets. Cover and leave in a warm place until the muffins have doubled in size. Bake in a hot oven (200°C, 400°F, gas mark 6) for 5 minutes. Turn the muffins and bake for a further five minutes.

Traditionally, muffins should not be split before toasting. They should be pulled open sightly at their joints, toasted back and front and then pulled open to butter the insides generously and served hot.

SANDWICHES

These should be dainty offerings. The bread should be fresh and moist, the crusts should be removed and the sandwiches cut into small rectangles. Variation is obtained by using different kinds of bread, different flavourings in the butters and different fillings. Check sandwiches are obtained by placing buttered brown and white slices (say 6) alternately on top of each other with different fillings between the slices and then cutting the pile into strips. (Butter the middle slices of bread on both sides.) Generally sandwiches keep well in polythene bags in the freezer. Use separate bags for different favours. The most traditional is the cucumber sandwich.

CUCUMBER SANDWICHES

Peel the cucumber and cut it into thin/transparent slices. Sprinkle with vinegar and a little salt and leave to stand for half an hour. Drain away excess cucumber juice. Lightly butter a paper-thin slice of brown bread and cover with two layers of cucumber slices. Place another buttered slice of brown bread on top. Press down gently. Remove the crusts and cut the sandwich into two rectangles. Repeat and pile the sandwiches on a plate. Cover with a damp cloth to keep them moist.

A traditional tea should begin with elegant savoury sandwiches followed by scones, buttered teabread, cream cakes, iced cakes, pastries and biscuits.
A cream tea consists of scones, clotted cream and strawberries.
The tea is usually China, Indian or a herb tea with milk or thin slices of lemon.
A rich fruit cake or cream cake extend an irresistible invitation as does the smell of toasted teacakes or muffins or crumpets and the clink of china cups.
High tea is usually more substantial and includes a savoury course.
But there is no set rule and teatime remains a welcome break in a shopping expedition or a time to relax, a pause before dinner and the evening.

SAVOURY AND SWEET BUTTERS

Some of these spreads are sufficient to make tasty sandwiches by themselves. Cream 100 g (4 oz) butter with any of the following:

12 anchovy fillets, lemon juice, a litle cayenne pepper and black pepper (for a milder flavour soak anchovies in milk for 20 minutes then drain)

12 boned sardines, 2 teaspoons Worcestershire sauce, salt and pepper

2 tablespoons flaked, poached salmon, 2 teaspoons lemon juice, salt and pepper

50 g (2 oz) chopped, cooked prawns, lemon juice, pepper

50 g (2 oz) prawns, pinch each grated nutmeg or mace and ground ginger, black pepper, salt, cayenne

2 tablespoons drained, chopped tuna, 1 tablespoon chopped cucumber, 1 tablespoon salad cream, pinch dry mustard, salt and pepper

4 tablespoons chopped watercress, 50 g (2 oz) cream cheese

2 tablespoons freshly chopped parsley, 1 teaspoon chopped chives, lemon juice, salt and black pepper

50 g (2 oz) crushed hazlenuts, 1 teaspoon brown sugar (use unsalted butter)

50 g (2 oz) toasted, unsalted almonds, pecan, walnuts, cashews (put nuts in a food processor with 1 tablespoon vegetable or sunflower oil and blend before creaming with the butter), salt

50 g (2 oz) unsalted peanuts (use 2 tablespoons peanut oil instead of butter and blend with the nuts in a food processor), salt

50 g (2 oz) brown sugar, 1 teaspoon powdered cinnamon, 1 tablespoon rum (use unsalted butter)

100 g (4 oz) caster sugar, 4 tablespoons brandy, 1 teaspoon lemon juice, 1 tablespoon boiling water (use unsalted butter)

100 g (4 oz) brown sugar, 4 tablespoons rum, 1 teaspoon orange juice, 1 tablespoon boiling water (use unsalted butter)

4 crushed cloves garlic, 1 tablespoon lemon juice, 1 teaspoon tabasco sauce, salt and white pepper

1 teaspoon each parsley, fennel fronds, chervil, basil, chopped chives, half crushed clove garlic, lemon juice, salt and pepper

2 tablespoons rosemary, tarragon or basil, 1 tablespoon chopped spring onions

2 tablespoons grated cheese, 2 tablespoons mixed pickle

SANDWICH FILLINGS

Ensure that the flavours of the filling and butter spread complement each other. If in doubt, use plain butter and not a flavoured one. Many of these fillings are excellent on toast.

Fillings
cream cheese, crushed walnuts
cream cheese, chopped chives, pickles
poached/tinned salmon, cucumber slices, lemon juice
boned, mashed sardines, watercress leaves, lemon juice
slice of cheese, grated apple, lemon juice
Danish Blue cheese, slices of pear, crushed walnuts, lemon juice
chopped ham, sliced tomato, chutney or pickles, mustard
chopped ham, Worcestershire sauce, cayenne pepper, French mustard, chopped parsley
prawns, mayonnaise, watercress leaves
flaked, smoked haddock, thick cream or mayonnaise, salt and pepper
lettuce, tomato, cheese, spring onion, grated carrot, salt and pepper
hard boiled egg mashed with 1 teaspoon thick cream or mayonnaise, watercress, salt and pepper
turkey or chicken, stuffing, cranberry sauce or bread sauce
salami, chopped onion
roast beef, mustard, pickles or lamb, mint sauce or bacon, cheese, tomato
sliced hard boiled egg, watercress
chopped, cooked bacon, chopped, hard boiled egg
mashed avocado, crushed pineapple, lemon juice
grated celery, crushed walnuts, thick cream, pinch cinnamon, sugar, salt and pepper
chopped smoked salmon, cream, whisky, grated nutmeg garnished with wafer thin slices of smoked salmon and served with wedges of lemon
poached, chopped mushrooms, Parmesan cheese, salt, pepper, cayenne

SAVOURIES

PRAWN AND MUSHROOM BITES

METRIC	IMPERIAL
24 vol-au-vents	24 vol-au-vents
milk	milk
Filling	**Filling**
6 tablespoons white wine	6 tablespoons white wine
75 g butter	3 oz butter
200 g button mushrooms	8 oz button mushrooms
400 g peeled prawns	1 lb peeled prawns
75 g plain flour	3 oz plain flour
600 ml milk	1 pint milk
300 ml double cream	½ pint double cream
200 g Gruyère or Emmental	8 oz Gruyère or Emmental
4 tablespoons Parmesan cheese	4 tablespoons Parmesan cheese
salt and pepper	salt and pepper
fresh parsley	fresh parsley
unshelled prawns	unshelled prawns

Brush the vol au vents with milk and bake in a moderately hot oven (200°C, 400°F, gas mark 6) for 10 - 15 minutes. Remove the tops and keep. Pour the wine into a saucepan and heat until the volume is reduced by half. Melt the butter in a large pan, add the mushrooms and prawns and fry gently heat for 5 minutes, stirring all the time. Remove the mushrooms and prawns on to kitchen paper. Work the flour into the liquid in the pan and heat for 1 - 2 minutes. Remove from the heat and blend in the milk, stirring to avoid the formation of lumps. Bring to the boil and simmer for 3 minutes until the sauce is thick and smooth. Season. Remove from the heat. Add the cream and wine, then the cheeses. Heat gently. Remove from the heat and add the prawns and mushrooms. Pour into the hot vol-au-vents. Replace the tops of the vol-au-vents and garnish with parsley and unshelled prawns. May also be served cold.

HAM AND PARMESAN BITES

Use the recipe for Prawn and Mushroom Bites on page 36. Omit the mushrooms, prawns and Gruyère or Emmental. Stir 100 g (4 oz) chopped, cooked ham and 2 tablespoons Parmesan cheese into the sauce.

DEVILLED HAM ON TOAST

METRIC
2 slices of hot toast
50 g lean ham (finely chopped)
2 teaspoons Worcestershire sauce
pinch of cayenne pepper
2 teaspoons French mustard
15 g butter
1 tablespoon chopped, fresh parsley

IMPERIAL
2 slices of hot toast
2 oz lean ham (finely chopped)
2 teaspoons Worcestershire sauce
pinch of cayenne pepper
2 teaspoons French mustard
½ oz butter
1 tablespoon chopped, fresh parsley

Mix the ham, Worcestershire sauce, cayenne pepper and French mustard together. Melt the butter and stir into the mixture. Heat the mixture gently. Remove the crusts from the toast. Place the ham mixture on the toast and garnish with parsley. Serve hot.

DEVILLED CHEESE ON TOAST

Mix 50 g (2 oz) grated Cheddar cheese and 1 tablespoon pickle. Spread on two rounds of toast and place under the grill until browned. Serve hot.

SEAFOOD QUICHE

METRIC
Flan cases
150 g plain flour
pinch salt
75 g butter
2 tablespoons cold water
Filling
150 g cooked, peeled prawns
1 tablespoon finely chopped shallots
1 tablespoon finely chopped parsley
1 tablespoon dry sherry
2 eggs (beaten)
250 ml single cream
pinch each nutmeg, salt, white pepper

IMPERIAL
Flan cases
6 oz plain flour
pinch salt
3 oz butter
2 tablespoons cold water
Filling
6 oz cooked, peeled prawns
1 tablespoon finely chopped shallots
1 tablespoon finely chopped parsley
1 tablespoon dry sherry
2 eggs (beaten)
¼ pint single cream
pinch each nutmeg, salt, white pepper

Flan cases Sift the flour and salt. Rub the butter into the flour until the mixture looks like breadcrumbs. Add the water and form into a firm dough. Roll out on a floured board. Cut into 7.5 cm (3 in) circles using a fluted pastry cutter and use to line six individual flan tins or deep patty tins. Bake blind as on page 26.

Filling Mix the prawns with the shallots, parsley and sherry. Leave to stand for 1 hour in the refrigerator. Sprinkle over the base of the flan cases. Whisk the eggs, cream, nutmeg, salt and white pepper together. Strain over the seafood in the flans and bake in a moderately hot oven (190ºC, 375ºF, gas mark 5) for 30 - 35 minutes until the filling is set and golden. Serve hot or cold with mixed salad. The quiche may also be made in a large round flan tin or a rectangular tin and sliced.

HERB QUICHE

Make the flan cases as in the recipe for Seafood Quiche. Sauté 8 shallots, finely chopped, in 2 tablespoons butter. Beat together two eggs and 250 ml (⅓ pint) cream. Stir in 1 tablespoon each chopped chives, chopped watercress, and chopped parsley, a pinch each salt and ground black pepper. Pour into the flan cases and bake in a moderately hot oven (190°C, 375°F, gas mark 5) for 30 - 35 minutes until the filling is set and golden. Serve hot or cold.

CHEESE AND BACON ROLLS

METRIC	IMPERIAL
200 g Cheddar cheese	*8 oz Cheddar cheese*
6 rashers of bacon	*6 rashers of bacon*

Cut the cheese into 2.5 cm (1 in) cubes. Remove rind and cut bacon into strips. Wrap the bacon strips around the cubes of cheese, securing with cocktail sticks. Cook under a grill, turning so that the bacon cooks before the cheese melts.

CHEESE PUDDING

METRIC	IMPERIAL
50 g grated Cheddar cheese	*2 oz grated Cheddar cheese*
300 ml milk	*⅓ pint milk*
50 g white breadcrumbs	*2 oz white breadcrumbs*
1 egg	*1 egg*
salt and pepper	*salt and pepper*

Boil the milk and pour over the breadcrumbs. Add the cheese. Season. Lightly beat the egg and add to the mixture. Pour into a lightly greased, ovenproof dish and bake in a moderately hot oven (190°C, 375°F, gas mark 5) for 30 minutes until golden brown. Serve with a mixed salad.

POTATO AND BACON PIE

METRIC
1 kilo potatoes
knob of butter
1 tablespoon milk
2 onions
1 cooking apple
6 slices of lean bacon
salt and pepper

IMPERIAL
2 lb potatoes
knob of butter
1 tablespoon milk
2 onions
1 cooking apple
6 slices of lean bacon
salt and pepper

Peel and boil the potatoes in salted water. Drain and mash with a little butter and milk. Skin and slice the onions. Cover with water in a saucepan and boil in salted water until soft. Peel, core and slice the apple. Grease a litre (2 pint) ovenproof pie dish. Put a layer of potato in the bottom of the dish then a layer of onion. Sprinkle lightly with pepper. Cover with a layer of apple. Top with potato and finally cover with the slices of bacon. Bake in a moderate oven (180°C, 350°F, gas mark 4) for 35 - 40 minutes until the bacon is cooked.

CORNED BEEF RISSOLES

Rissoles: Mix together mashed, boiled potatoes, corned beef, chopped onion, breadcrumbs, a pinch of mixed herbs, and a dash of Worcestershire sauce. Season. Bind with beaten egg or milk. Form into patties 5.7 cm (3 inches) across and 1 cm (half an inch) thick. Dip in seasoned flour and fry in a little vegetable oil or butter. Serve with salad.
Seasoned flour: Sift a little salt and white pepper with the flour.

c. 1875

BISCUITS

SHORTBREAD FINGERS

METRIC
100 g butter
50 g caster sugar
150 g plain flour
25 g ground rice

IMPERIAL
4 oz butter
2 oz caster sugar
6 oz plain flour
1 oz ground rice

Cream the butter and sugar together until light and fluffy. Stir in the flour and ground rice. Knead into a pliable paste. Roll out on a greased surface until the dough is just over 0.5 cm (¼ in) thick. Cut into fingers 7.5 x 2 cm (3 x ¾ in). Place on a greased baking sheet, cover and cool in the refrigerator for 30 minutes. Bake in a moderately hot oven (190ºC, 375ºF, gas mark 5) for 25 minutes until golden brown. Dust with caster sugar while still warm.

ORANGE AND LEMON SHORTBREAD FINGERS

Using the recipe for Shortbread Fingers, stir 1 teaspoon each finely grated orange rind and lemon rind into the mixture with the flour.

GINGER/CINNAMON SHORTBREAD FINGERS

Using the recipe for Shortbread Fingers, stir 1 teaspoon ground ginger **or** ground cinnamon into the mixture with the flour.

CRUNCHY OATMEAL SQUARES

METRIC	IMPERIAL
100 g butter	*4 oz butter*
75 g rolled oats	*3 oz rolled oats*
75 g desiccated coconut	*3 oz desiccated coconut*
75 g demerara sugar	*3 oz demerara sugar*
½ teaspoon vanilla essence	*½ teaspoon vanilla essence*
75 g dried mixed fruit	*3 oz dried mixed fruit*

Grease a 32.5 x 22.5 cm (13 x 9 in) Swiss roll tin. Melt the butter and stir in the oats, coconut, sugar, vanilla essence and fruit. Turn into the baking tin and spread evenly. Bake in a moderate oven (180ºC, 350ºF, gas mark 4) for 30 - 40 minutes until firm. While still warm cut into squares.

CHOCOLATE DROPS

METRIC	IMPERIAL
100 g butter	*4 oz butter*
50 g caster sugar	*2 oz caster sugar*
100 g self raising flour	*4 oz self raising flour*
pinch of salt	*pinch of salt*
25 g drinking chocolate powder	*1 oz drinking chocolate powder*
50 g plain chocolate	*2 oz plain chocolate*

Lightly grease a baking sheet. Cream the butter and sugar together until they are light and fluffy. Sift the flour, salt and chocolate powder together and fold into the creamed mixture. Form into small balls about 2.5 cm (1 in) in diameter and place on the baking sheet. Leave room for the biscuits to spread a little. Flatten the tops slightly using a knife moistened with water. Bake in a moderately hot oven (180ºC, 350ºF, gas mark 4) for 8 - 10 minutes. Leave on the tray for 1 minute. Melt the plain chocolate in a bowl standing over hot water. Sandwich the biscuits together in pairs with the melted chocolate.

JAMS

WHOLE STRAWBERRY CONSERVE

METRIC
1 kilo small strawberries
3 tablespoons lemon juice
1 kilo granulated sugar
knob of butter
200 ml pectin

IMPERIAL
2 lb small strawberries
3 tablespoons lemon juice
2 lb granulated sugar
knob of butter
¼ pint pectin

Wash and hull the strawberries. Place in a bowl with the lemon juice and sugar. Mix well. Cover and leave to stand for 1 hour. Pour into a pan and heat slowly, stirring until the sugar dissolves. Add the butter. Bring to the boil and boil rapidly for 4 minutes, stirring occasionally. Remove from the heat and stir in the pectin. Cover and leave to stand for 20 minutes. Pot and seal in warm, sterilised jars.

STRAWBERRY/RASPBERRY JAM

Wash and hull 4 lb (2 kilo) strawberries or raspberries. Crush the fruit using a fork. Stir in 4 lb (2 kilo) caster sugar and 5 tablespoons lemon juice. Cover and leave to stand for 1 hour. Stir in 200 ml (¼ pint) pectin. Mix well, stirring gently. Pour into freezer containers, close and leave at room temperature for 24 hours. Place in freezer and keep for up to 6 months.

BLACKBERRY AND APPLE JAM

METRIC
2 kilo blackberries

300 ml water
1 kilo cooking apples
2 kilo granulated sugar
knob of butter

IMPERIAL
4 lb blackberries

½ pint water
2 lb cooking apples
6 lb granulated sugar
knob of butter

Wash the blackberries. Simmer gently in half the water. Sieve to remove seeds. Peel, core and slice the apples. Heat in the remaining water until the fruit is soft. Mash. Mix the apple pulp and blackberry purée together and stir in the sugar until it has dissolved. Add the knob of butter. Bring the jam to the boil and boil rapidly for ten minutes until the setting point is reached. Take the pan away from the heat and remove any scum from the surface. Pot in sterilised jars and seal.

Setting point: Put a little of the jam on a cold saucer and leave to cool. Push a finger gently through it. If the surface wrinkles, setting point has been reached (approximately 105°C, 221°F). **Remove the pan from the heat while doing the test so that the temperature does not rise too high.**

LEMON CURD

METRIC
Grated rind and juice of 2 large lemons
50 g butter
150 g caster sugar
2 eggs

IMPERIAL
Grated rind and juice of 2 large lemons
2 oz butter
6 oz caster sugar
2 eggs

Heat rind, juice, butter and sugar in a double saucepan. Blend in the eggs, one at a time, and beat well. Warm and stir until the mixture is thick and creamy. Pot in sterilised jars and seal.

RELISHES

SPICY APPLE RELISH

METRIC	IMPERIAL
Chutney	*Chutney*
1 kilo cooking apples (peeled, cored and chopped)	*2 lb cooking apples (peeled, cored and chopped)*
4 oz sultanas	*100 g sultanas*
2 large onions (skinned and chopped)	*2 large onions (skinned and chopped)*
1 clove garlic (chopped)	*1 clove garlic (chopped)*
100 g sugar	*4 oz sugar*
1 teaspoon salt	*1 teaspoon salt*
2 teaspoons each ground ginger, dry mustard	*2 teaspoons each ground ginger, dry mustard*
pinch of cayenne pepper	*pinch of cayenne pepper*
50 g dates (chopped)	*2 oz dates (chopped)*
50 g preserved ginger (chopped)	*2 oz preserved ginger (chopped)*
Spiced vinegar	*Spiced vinegar*
600 ml white vinegar	*1 pint white vinegar*
2 teaspoons black peppercorns	*2 teaspoons black peppercorns*
1 teaspoon each mustard seeds, whole allspice	*1 teaspoon each mustard seeds, whole allspice*
2 teaspoons brown sugar	*2 teaspoons brown sugar*

Spiced vinegar Place all the ingredients in an enamel saucepan, bring to the boil. Remove from the heat and leave to cool. Strain.

Chutney Add all the ingredients to the strained spiced vinegar. Mix well using a wooden spoon and simmer gently for about 1 ½ hours until thick. Spoon into sterilised jars and seal.

PLUM AND TOMATO RELISH

METRIC
800 g plums
800 g red tomatoes
900 ml malt vinegar
2 cloves garlic
400 g onions
1 kg apples
200 g mixed dried fruit
400 g demerara sugar
4 teaspoons salt
1 tablespoon pickling spice

IMPERIAL
2 lb plums
2 lb red tomatoes
1 ¼ pints malt vinegar
2 cloves garlic
1 lb onions
2 lb apples
8 oz mixed dried fruit
1 lb demerara sugar
4 teaspoons salt
1 tablespoon pickling spice

Wash the plums, halve and remove stones. Immerse the tomatoes in hot water to loosen the skins. Place the plums, skinned tomatoes and vinegar in a large pan and simmer until soft. Skin and chop the garlic and onions. Peel, core and slice the apples. Tie the pickling spice in a piece of muslin. Add all the ingredients to the pan. Stir well using a wooden spoon. Simmer gently for about 2 hours, stirring occasionally until the mixture is reduced and thick. Remove the bag of spices. Pot in sterilized jars and seal.

c. 1715

AMERICAN MEASURES

American measures are given by volume and weight using standard cups and spoons.

US Standard Measuring Spoons and Cups

1 tablespoon = 3 teaspoons = ½ fluid ounce = 14.2 ml
2 tablespoons = 1 fluid ounce = 28 ml
4 tablespoons = ¼ cup
5 tablespoons = ⅓ cup
8 tablespoons = ½ cup
10 tablespoons = $\frac{2}{3}$ cup
12 tablespoons = ¾ cup
16 tablespoons = 2 cups = 8 fluid ounces = ½ US pint
32 tablespoons = 2 cups = 16 fluid ounces = 1 US pint.

Metric (Imperial)	American
1 teaspoon	1 teaspoon
1 tablespoon	1 tablespoon
1½ teaspoons	2 tablespoons
2 tablespoons	3 tablespoons
3 tablespoons	¼ (scant) cup
4 tablespoons	5 tablespoons
5 tablespoons	6 tablespoons
5½ tablespoons	7 tablespoons
6 tablespoons (scant ¼ pint)	½ cup
¼ pint	$\frac{2}{3}$ cup
scant ½ pint	1 cup
½ pint (10 fl oz)	1¼ cups
¾ pint (15 fl oz)	scant 2 cups
¾ pint (16 fl oz)	2 cups (1 pint)
1 pint (20 fl oz)	2½ cups

Metric (Imperial)	American
flour, plain or self-raising	
15 g (½ oz)	2 tablespoons
25 g (1 oz)	1½ cup
100/125 g (4 oz)	1 cup
sugar, caster or granulated, brown (firmly packed)	
25 g (1 oz)	2 tablespoons
100/125 g (4 oz)	½ cup
200/225 g (8 oz)	1 cup
butter, margarine, fat	
1 oz	2 tablespoons
225 g (8 oz)	1 cup
150 g (5 oz) shredded suet	1 cup

1 cup (American) contains approximately
100/125 g (4 oz) grated cheese, 50 g (2 oz) fresh breadcrumbs,
100 g (4 oz) dried breadcrumbs,
100/125 g (4 oz) pickled beetroot, button mushrooms, shelled peas, red/blackcurrants, 5 oz strawberries,
175 g (6 oz) raisins, currants, sultanas, chopped candied peel, stoned dates,
225 g (8 oz) glacé cherries, 150 g (5 oz) shelled whole walnuts,
100 g (4 oz) chopped nuts,
75 g (3 oz) desiccated coconut,
225 g (8 oz) cottage cheese,
100/125 g (4 oz) curry powder,
225 g (8 oz) minced raw meat,
$\frac{3}{8}$ pint (7½ fl oz) cream.

INDEX